02/04
17.95

The Road to the
Gunpowder House

Neil Curry

The Road to the Gunpowder House

ENITHARMON PRESS

First published in 2003
by the Enitharmon Press
26B Caversham Road
London NW5 2DU

www.enitharmon.co.uk

Distributed in the UK by
Central Books
99 Wallis Road
London E9 5LN

Distributed in the USA and Canada
by Dufour Editions Inc.
PO Box 7, Chester Springs
PA 19425, USA

ISBN 1 900564 28 9

British Library Cataloguing-in-Publication Data.
A catalogue record for this book is available
from the British Library

Typeset in Bembo by Servis Filmsetting Ltd
and printed in England by
Antony Rowe Ltd

for my wife
Peggy

ACKNOWLEDGEMENTS

Some of these poems first appeared in the following publications: *Acumen, Blue Notes, Defined Providence, Hasty Magazine, Illuminations, Island, Making Connections, Orbis, Pitch, Poems 25, Poetry Ireland, Poetry London, Red Herring, Stand, The Edge, The London Magazine, The Reader, The Rialto, Tracks, Scintilla, Write Now.*

My thanks also go to the Djerassi Resident Artists Program, The Blue Mountain Center, and Yaddo.

CONTENTS

IV

V

'. . . they that do business
in great waters'

Tap-tapping with his pencil
like Blind Pew,
it crossed his mind how often
words had led him into areas
as menacing and unmapped
as any of the polar wastes
the likes of Frobisher
and Franklin sailed to.

So fragile their barques,
ambition chafed against survival.
Could iron and creaking oak
hold out against water,
wind and ice; compass
and chart contend
with snow and fog; could
ingenuity outwit this wild?

Certain shallow bays and attendant
headlands having been found
and named, they headed for home.
Crouching in their cabins, their journals
cradled against the pitch
and yaw, they searched for words
to relate the groaning
of the floes, the winds' howling.

I

TIDELINES
(HOLY ISLAND)

> — the swan's down feather,
> That stands upon the swell at full tide,
> And neither way inclines.
>> *Antony and Cleopatra* III.ii.48–50

1

Beginnings can be difficult.
Even so, had I begun with that line
in the days of Eadfrith, Cuthbert, Bede,
I wouldn't have got this far yet.
I'd still be pricking vellum for my initial
B; letting the plump O's of it
billow out over the page, and its long stem
fall further and further down the edge
like a mare's tail, like kelp, like candlewax,
like some thick, round, midwinter icicle.

2

You've seen the way a sheepdog
comes across a field with that low,
rippling, crouching sort of run they have,
threatening a nip to every jostling
heel of the flock they're driving?
Well, this morning's neap tide was like that,
menacing its way over the mudflats
and setting up such a panic
among the sandpiper, plover and knot
that they were all flickering in and out
of the lacings and leavings of it
as if nothing quite like this
had ever happened to them before.

3

This, naturally, would have been nothing new
to any apprentice of Eadfrith. His rule
ran as inexorably as the tides:
the tablets of wax their craft was learned on
needed to be pristine smooth again
each morning: interlace went the way
of worm-casts; vowels and consonants
like footprints of the birds. Sound practice,
he insisted, likewise a lesson in humility.
Nothing lasts in this world. What was it he'd seen once
doodled down a margin somewhere: 'Whirl is King!'?

4

plant becomes fish
fish beast and beast bird
in this gorgeous zoomorphic
interlace of spiral and curve
branch feather and fin
interwoven in a celebration
of creation where we can see
plant become fish
fish beast and beast bird
in this gorgeous zoomorphic
interlace of spiral and curve
branch feather and fin
interwoven in a celebration
of creation where we can see
plant become fish

5

For all that it's axe-shaped,
flourishing its blade in the face of the North Sea,
Lindisfarne succumbs, must give ground
twice a day as the waters come in
over the causeway, and cut it off.
And not only in space – time too.
This afternoon there is no past here – no *harrying*
of the heathen in these invasions of the tide;
it's just water, just the rattle and drag
of shingle, something that's happening now.

6

Far out, a wave is little more than a slight
darkening of the water, a suspicion
of shadow, a deepening of the blue
that swells slowly, growing into a grey
wall of water that rises and rises until it's
so high it over-reaches itself, topples
and falls, breaking into fragments of foam.

7

So much cobble and shingle. Sandstone
I can recognise – granite and slate. And over there's
what's surely a piece of smoothed-off
building brick; but these others, the dull, round
grey ones – they must have names too. And down among the grit
and gravel (never mind the shells) there's such
carmine and cadmium, such amber and
(who knows?) pearl, and not one bit of it
altogether accident – each with a history
of the collisions and contingencies
that have broken, shaped and burnished them,
as they judder backwards and forwards
between the grandeur and futility of it all.

They could be eider: Cuddy's ducks,
but with this low-sun, high-wind
faceting of the waves it's hard to tell;
in fact it's hard to settle on anything
with these gusts of gulls being
blown about across a mackerel sky.
Whirl, it seems, is truly king today.

Looking over towards the low
outline of Hob Thrush, Cuthbert's Island,
the stories surface; as otters did
coming out of the sea to warm
and dry his feet after he'd stood
all night praying waist-deep
in the waves off Coldingham;

and those ravens, thatch-thieves,
bringing him lumps of lard in recompense
to waterproof his boots. Stories
that keep their hold on us
but drove him, with their risk
of fame, to his beehive hermitage
on Inner Farne, and the sky and the sea,

and the sea and the dry land. Balanced
on this margin and threshold of the world,
he could hold out against the tidal
pull and push of self – his life pared and honed so
it flourished among the thrift and samphire,
Peter's herb, along the shoreline: moments
stilled to rock-pools where the small

quick shadows of translucent things
scurried under stones – a stasis so total
and complete the sea itself could not
compete with it, though I saw it try once
in Rusland Pool: the tide
wrestling against the strength of the river
and the river fighting to hold it back,

and for perhaps half a minute it seemed
they called a truce – such a calm
settled, it was as if the present
had overlapped both past and future:
the swan's down feather. But the river,
catching the sea off guard began nudging it slowly
back again to where it rightfully belongs.

Barefoot we crossed the sands to Lindisfarne.

II

THE ALHAMBRA, GRANADA

Once at least it seemed to them,
the navigators and explorers,
(it was in the South Arabian seas
where the scent of aloes reached them
on an offshore breeze)
that they'd come very close to finding Eden,

but when finally they gave up in despair,
agreeing, what ought
to have been obvious from the start,
that the Flood had doubtless swept
all trace of it away,
then one by one their patrons,

men of imagination and of wealth,
decided it was time to build,
each for himself, a paradise on earth,
so the ships were all laid up,
maps stowed away and gardeners sought
to re-create that home

their hearts all hungered for,
where they could enjoy the shade
of their own vines, breathe in the fragrance
of jasmine and hear the splash
of fountains in the evening;
the ancient feeling of estrangement overcome

at last, and put to rest
with never a wilting leaf
or any of entropy's transactions
permitted to intrude
on what might otherwise have proved
to be such a good place to die in.

Shears and secateurs are in command here:
any extravagant inclination towards growth
gets clipped right back into line. Order prevails

in a controlled opulence, which His Eminence
perhaps saw as being yet one more triumph
over chaos, where whatsoever was barbaric,

or hostile, or simply less than perfect
had been wisely, firmly and finally walled out.
From the top of the grand staircase it is still

possible to catch a glimpse of the Campagna,
but on the way down our eyes are held
by alleys of gravel, scroll-works of box,

hard-edged laurel, ilex and yew; and stone,
stone everywhere: stone walls, stone benches,
terraces with balustrades and statues,

fountains, where water is flung time and again
high into the air and sculpted into fantasies.
Less the work of gardeners than of

architects, outdoors here seems to be only
one more aspect of what went on indoors,
and pre-eminently an assertion of will,

a symbol of power. Twice though,
having lost our way on a lower level,
we came face to face with the same defunct

fountain, left to dribble over what might once
have been Bacchus, but now had become a green
grotesque: slime running down its belly;

a rank stench of mildew; lichen and moss
sprouting out of his nose, his ears, his mouth. We both
knew him in an instant; knew that the Green Man
had somehow climbed back in over the wall.

It's early days yet in the Cool House:
there are new ferns with their heads curled
as tight as croziers, while others,
taking after the horsetails are not only
up, but already so rampant
we look like having the whole
of the primeval swamp here soon in bonsai.

Being a gathering together, it would seem,
of the scattered shards of that First Eden,
this rhetorical landscape does not preserve
only what's pretty – hence the sundew
that upset Ruskin so, and the deadly dewlap
of the Pitcher Plant, some kinds of which, it's said,
trap and digest small reptiles, even rats –

or only what's exotic: it is oddly
reassuring to come across rhubarb here,
but to find a dandelion is somehow shocking;
usually they grow at the whim of the wind,
in the lawn, or in cracks between paving stones;
this one though has a nameplate all its own
so demands that it be looked at, not just seen,

that we try to recognise the truth
of it, not the truth about it; responding
to its sheer incandescent explosion
of yellow, yet, at the same time, aware
that each individual petal
is straight-edged as a chisel. Being
uncertain is what mostly makes us

wonder. Seldom permitted
the chance simply to look, we know
what's coming; and in this case it's
the geometrical miracle of that seed head,
the blow-away clock. There is no
such thing as immaculate perception
where everything's myth, everywhere caprice.

We cannot all have our gardens
now, nor our pleasant fields to
meditate in at eventide.
The Stones of Venice

Skies, Ruskin once confessed,
he bottled with the same care
his father used when bottling sherries;
but when the air went still
and he could sense
the thunderheads gathering
on the other side of the hill,
it was himself he bottled up in Brantwood.

Standing at his window
on long December afternoons,
he watched the changing
colours of the mist –
topaz, amethyst, jade –
smouldering on the surface of the lake;
but if, as he was to insist,
there is 'no wealth but life'

then that house of his down there,
squat and prim,
with its straight-jacket cot
in an upstairs room,
and all those useless
collections of stones
must have been
nigh on beggary.

Yes, that was when I made my very first tree.
  Feeling it inside me was simply not enough.
Those branches though – what a surprise they were.
  They were my tree over again a thousand times.
I am, of course, a part of all that I create,
  But I'd never known what it was to be in leaf
Until suddenly there I stood giving shade,
  Birds fluttering all around my head.
My omnipotence surging in its sap,
  My trunk seemed to stretch up to the skies,
But the ground had my roots held fast in its trap.
  It was then that I made my very first tree.
And man came and sat beneath my leaves;
  So innocent he was and so new.
It was an oak, I think – or an elm perhaps.
  It's hard to tell now; it's all so long ago.
But I do remember how it pleased the man.
  He fell asleep there with a smile round his eyes,
And in his dreams he was walking through a wood,
  So as soon as he woke I built him a forest,
Instantly ancient with enormous trees
  And three hundred stags galloping about,
Each with its hind and each hind with its fawn,
  Galloping through those trees as though they'd always been.
The air was loud with the belling of the bucks.
  New-born they were, yet wide-antlered and in rut.
From their first breath their hearts were full of hope
  And their heads with memories that had once been mine.
At a word then I made the pine, the spruce, the ash,
  With squirrels scampering in their topmost twigs.
I made the little boy who weeps because he's lost,
  And a kindly woodsman to show him the way.

Heaven though I concealed as closely as I could;
  Its distances are much too much for man.
But on some bright mornings he may glimpse it yet,
  When birds are singing and the grass feels wet.

(Jules Supervielle)

TOUCH WOOD

Touch Wood, we say,
hoping it'll bring us luck,
and as luck would have it, today
I have only to put down my book,
and step outside to be *in* a wood:
sycamore and ash, maple and oak
and no two trees ever the same.

Trees don't even burn the same.
Some are generous with their heat,
but give it out slowly,
while others crackle and spit sparks
so in next to no time you're outside
filling the log-basket up again.

Their bark can be so different too:
from the scaly furrows of the larch
to the smooth, dark grey of the beech –
beech being a name that shares
the same root (notice the metaphor)
as the Old English word for *book*.
No, we're not out of the woods yet.

In Ireland I was told the first man
came from an alder tree, the first
woman from the rowan or mountain ash;
and once there was a law that anyone
who did violence to a tree
should be decapitated on its stump.

Trees outlive us, and we envy them
their permanence. There never was
a tree that looked unsightly, and nothing
else on earth can be said
to still look beautiful when it's dead.

It's when trees do die though
that they can sometimes
be a tad erratic: playing host
to so many different kinds of fungus –
some like frost and some like toffee-apples.
One I saw looked as crusty
as a new brown loaf
and beside it was a tiny blob
the colour of ripe cheddar.

And they are the trees that fall.
Those that are felled, dried
and seasoned get cherished
lovingly. Sawn and planed
to a finish that's silken to the thumb,
they are the ones that furnish our lives,
the ones that will outlast us, and the ones
which may, mercifully, one day become
a coffin for relatives to hide
our own unlovely putrefaction in.
Touch wood.

WOOD-SORREL

Petite (in the way we English
use the word) it is;
a white, five-petalled cup, lightly
veined with lilac,
eye-catching though, coming out so early
among the litter of last year's dead leaves;

hinged or moth-winged, its leaves recoil,
folding up in wet
weather into something like the
pinched crown of an
Anzac hat, or a priest's biretta. Chewed on,
their bright taste is an acidy-lemon,

so the name it was given was
wood-sorrel. Of course
some saw it differently. Gerard
in his *Herball*
called it Cuckowe's Meat, 'by reason that when
it springeth forth, the Cuckow singeth most.'

Then there were all those other names:
the Alleluya
Flower, Green Sauce, Lady's Clover;
the exotic
and the enigmatic, together with
some as endearingly improbable

as God Almighty's Bread and Cheese:
each, in its own way,
bringing with it the signature
of previous
encounters, of our place in its context,
of its standing in our complexity.

Orange lilies are flowering through my desk
here in upstate New York, and the overhead
lamp is a harvest moon entangled
in the branches of that silver birch,

and the uncomfortable armchair –
the biscuit-coloured one I never sit in –
is levitating above where the lawn slopes down
to the lake. The fireplace is out there too.

And so am I. I am looking at myself,
sitting at my desk in the garden,
oblivious to the rain; just sitting there,
staring in here where it's dry.

Precedence is hard to reconcile.
Earlier, when I was looking at the hills
beyond the lake, they slid away, and there was
Morecambe Bay – and the tide was out

and Chapel Island, as always, was looking
as if it had run aground and was waiting
to be floated off again, and I
could hear the cries of the gulls,

the high piping of the oyster catchers,
and that sustained E flat
the little green flies hold onto
as they hover over the warm bracken.

WILLIAM AND ADAM

No one could claim they've had it easy,
William and Adam, the two
chubby-legged stone cherubs
now gracing our narrow, damp back garden.

They could never have imagined themselves
ending up like this: on their uppers
one might say, if they had any.

Two hundred years ago
would have seen them glancing shyly out
from some herbaceous border,
wide-crinolined Cassandras
and Carolines floating by.

What a come-down.

Even so, they've known worse.
Both at some time
had their heads knocked off:
an anti-cherubic faction
of the *sans-culottes* maybe.

But then things did get better.
Someone, seeing their plight, took pity
and mended them, so cack-handedly though
(which is why we got them cheap)
that each now looks to be wearing
a concrete woolly muffler round his neck.

They need them too in this weather.
After breakfast I noticed
the trumpet of a daffodil
resting against William's ear
like an old-time telephone;
and Adam, that winsome smile of his,
turned towards him, suggesting:
'I think it might be someone for me.'

III

III

A Mandate

To all intents he was a tender gardener.
He turned the soil, secured the trellis
to the wall, and twined the tendrils

of the seedling sweet-peas through it
as they grew; yet he himself was up
and gone before the hawthorn was in bloom,

and heading westwards (the candles
of the sweet-peas flickered out and died)
and then still west and west again

until it came to him some flowers he passed
he'd never seen before, like this small yellow one:
with something of the poppy to it,

but only half the size, yet not a celandine.
And the birds, even the little brown birds,
he couldn't name: it was a locale

rinsed of the accretions of habit,
of innuendo, even of surmise; somewhere
waiting to be seen for what it is;

as if Adam had been allowed back into Eden
with a pocket full of labels, and a mandate
that he re-enchant the world.

Not a complete shell, just a broken
water-polished piece of one, but the more
precious for that, being all I could find,

so I brought it back to put alongside
the blue-jay's feather and the acorns
I picked up while out walking yesterday.

Why we keep on doing this it's hard to tell.
These acorns I like, I know, because of
the raggedy-knitted berets that they wear,

but in themselves, the stones, the feathers
and the sprigs of lichen are nothing special.
Maybe we re-invent them; allow

them meanings; or slowly they tell us
what their meanings are; metaphors, or icons
possibly: somewhere a god might be

persuaded, or engage to come. They come
and go of course: lichens crumble, and stones
tend somedays to look much like stones.

Some may become things we can't be parted from,
but they too get put out with the rubbish
by strangers or by daughters when we die.

ROCK POOLS

You have to have patience
in your dealings with the sea:
only walking along beside it quietly
for an hour or so
can ready you for its rock pools.

Today a hermit-crab had left
a needlepoint of tracks
in the sand outside a whelk shell –
a channelled whelk I think it's called –
old gold, whitened with a wash of salt.

The mouth looked puffed and swollen
but was opalescent and smooth inside,
with its wide skirts winding up
in gentle, tightening spirals.
It seemed best then to just let it be,

but now I wish I had it here to hold.
There are times when memories are not enough
and neither are poems, even when the words,
having come so close to what we cannot say,
gather themselves slowly around the silence.

Something's upset them.
As ever, the redshanks – with four or five little
high-pitched shrieks and trills –
are the first to be up and off;
then it's the dunlin, knit tight
as a shoal of herring; flickerings
of white – aspen leaves in a high wind –
each time the flock dips and turns.

Did they see it, or sense it?
I've only this moment
made out what it is myself.

A peregrine, coming like a small black
anchor flung across the sky,
slows,
rolls and climbs,
looking for some unlucky loner,
then stoops.

Locked onto its target it follows
every desperate lunge and dive,
answers every jink and sprint.
But it's no contest.
This is a Viking
got in among the monks,
the marriage of predator and prey.

One small puff of feathers and it's finished.

For a moment, a few hang
in the empty air,
then drizzle down slowly
over the waves.

Something is dead . . .

>   *nor was it*
> *thought possible that such*
> *an inroad from the sea could be made.*

Silence.

Then tentative
pitch-pipe sounds are heard.

The rest of us are still alive.

Minor volcanic
disturbances apart,
things tended to be fairly

quiet in Pangaea. Occasional
quakes and consequent
tsunami might result in some

slight re-shaping,
but nothing tectonic: small
break-aways perhaps, little

fallings-off that sank
almost immediately. One or two,
caught by a fortunate

trade wind drifted off
slowly east, to be drenched
in the scents of cinnamon

and clove. And then there was no
stopping it. Before long
there seemed to be whaling ships

and libraries almost everywhere.
In campsites on the edges
of the wilderness there were also

rumours of Atlantis, said to be
fabulous, but though often
talked about, it was never found.

This is where it begins:
this footbridge over the throat of the estuary,
where the Crake and the Leven roil
under the inrush of the tide,
and pale swirls of ochre silt come rising up
to explode and blossom in the flow.

The hawthorn isn't yet in flower,
but there are catkins out on the hazels,
and the other side of the river,
in Roudsea Wood,
where the path bends to the right,
you get an earlier glimpse of the shoreline
since that broad stand of timber
has been felled and cleared.

It's always quiet here.
Thick wads of felt were tied to the hooves
of the horses hauling the wagons
up and down this track:
one struck spark would have been enough.

But that's all dead and done with now:
gunpowder, horses, mines.
The four-square, stout-walled powderhouse
has been reformed into a rustic somewhere
for the Cavendish to host
a summer evening's barbecue.

Through the windows you see logs
piled tidily by the fireplace, wicker chairs
and bottles choked with gutterings of wax.
The door's been shut tight all winter.
Some eavesdropping spider
has spun a web across the keyhole.
It too is alive
to the possibilities of explosion.

OVID IN EXILE

Late afternoon
until early evening, as on every other
late afternoon and early evening,
he stood and watched the waves,
one after another, shuffling unstoppably ashore.

Mere cats' paws they were mostly,
but nine such, he'd been warned,
unleashed a tenth with tow enough
to maul and claw you under.

Well, and why not?
One's exit should have some panache;
and better that than the peremptory
botch-up they'd likely give him in Tomis.

Exile. As if getting old
weren't exile enough in itself;
though he of all people surely
should have spotted that metamorphosis coming.

Memories ambushed his mind:
how her wind-teased tresses turned to green leaves
as Apollo's hands reached out
to take her; strands become twigs
and Daphne safely and forever laurel.

Now there were no trees, and no girls either.
What he had instead was what he thought
he'd always wanted, and that was time.

Like a thing taken for granted,
the earth turned through a blizzard of stars.

Time – that plumps the grape
but dulls the plough – he'd wasted
looking for ships; waiting for letters;
he might as well have tried to till the sand,
littered as it was with shells, the way words
littered his lines; pretty to look at,
but the life gone out of them.

A curlew called from the dunes.

As he'd said to Severus once:
writing a poem with no one to read it
was like dancing in the dark.

A finger of cloud smudged out the moon.

But what could he do?
He clapped his hands and he shuffled
his feet, and he danced – danced
like a man garnering the sun.

Why of course. There wasn't the slightest
hesitation. A mother and child
might very well (yes, Mrs Ramsay even,
sitting at her window)
be reduced, she rattled on,
to a triangular purple shadow,
just there, just there, you see,
without demeaning them.

Each mass, each highlight, depth and texture
required the balance of its counterpoint.
She began to sense herself believing this.
And so reality
was what you made of it. James
was slowly prising loose a flake of paint
with his fingernail
while his mother read

aloud to him in the fisherman's
gruff voice, and Lily, out there in the garden,
stood quiet now, beside her easel,
wishing for one of those
moments which, by running
so very counter to reality,
had somehow almost
reconciled her to it.

And having dibbed and dabbled long enough
among the umbers and the blues, she raised
her brush, held it poised, and like an angel
on a pinhead tried
to balance, even to dance
a few light steps upon it, but she failed.
'Women can't paint.' Why then
persist, teetering on

jostled so by such inconsequence?
A skimpy little thing, she'd heard one say,
who'd never marry and would never sit
like Mrs Ramsay
in a window seat,
her son upon her lap and read to him.
No one would ensconce her
in a purple shadow.

And so she wiped her brushes on a rag
and tidied everything away. And as she did
she sang a little to herself, quite wordlessly,
but they heard her, and heard
how through the rhythms
of what might otherwise have proved a dirge,
she intertwined some grace notes
of incorrigible hope.

ATTICS

One of my ambitions is to have lived
as a child in a house with an attic,
the sort you get to up a narrow
wooden staircase – bare boards, no carpet –
the sort of staircase with a sharp bend in it
just five or six steps below a shabby door
that swings shut behind you on its sneck

attics are where things end up that no one
wants, but no one thinks to throw away:
boxes of photographs, long-tasselled lampshades,
a tennis racquet with a fish-tail handle

attics are where bachelor uncles
who went abroad, never to return,
left behind their *personal possessions*

attics are where stories start, where letters
are found, and lonely, sensitive children
make discoveries about themselves

I will, it seems, have missed out on this,
driving to the tip with bits and pieces
I could have safely stowed upstairs,
to be stumbled on sometime by someone
who would laugh and call out, 'You really have
to take a look at this,' or quietly
to themselves, say, 'Oh, now I understand.'

Dreams had been playing
at ducks and drakes with her
half the night, skittering her
in and out of shallow sleep,

until at last she'd given in
and come downstairs,
leant back against the doorway,
propped one foot up behind her,

settled her shoulders and folded
her arms. Not a pose Vermeer
would have favoured, more
of a Murillo; not that it mattered,

not when the entire garden
looked to have re-composed itself
in the time it had taken her
to unlatch the door.

Moon-bleached, it was so still,
so quiet and so new. What had been
weeds were wild flowers,
flowering wildly among the scented

pomp of bloom and trimmed box.
An unlooked-for grace it was,
she felt, to be there at all,
and by herself, able to just stand

and look at this thing
or at that: the sun rising;
a billhook left out overnight
in the wet grass; the blood

and rust of dahlias by the path.
A moment to treasure. Nothing
unusual, nothing . . . hadn't she
heard somewhere the first

dahlias had come from Mexico?
That they'd been Aztec flowers?
Those painted priests, frightful
in their feathers, had her held down

and were reaching for the billhook
when the peacock morning
screamed out before her and she
was on her feet, brushing something

off her skirt, as sunlight
ruffled her hair and from the kitchen
came the smell of toast
and the sound of coffee being made.

Sitting at the little outdoor café
she mostly favoured, Valeska's,
on the corner of the Träumenstrasse,
its six blue tables each with a
tall glass vase of dwarf delphinium,

she found she couldn't settle;
if she wasn't fingering her scarf
she was twizzling her spoon about
inside her cup, or cutting her pastry
into tiny cubes. Too many of her mornings

were tending to begin this way of late:
she might have been an actress
standing in the wings, waiting, anxious,
listening for a cue that never came.
But a triumphant carillon

then rang out, bang on cue, and she glanced up
just in time to see a shock-head David
jump from a Gothic door and punctually
slay Goliath, as the clock in the tower
of the Rathaus chimed the hour.

And she thought how, if she could
only freeze and fix one moment,
mount it as one would a butterfly
so as to study it, to take a long
close look at it, complete

in its totality, that would make
all the difference, would make sense
of the most ordinary of things:
the patterns the starlings made when they
exploded like scatter-shot from the roof-tops

would then become to her as treasures
salvaged from a shipwrecked dream.
But they were already settling back
on every gable end; clouds had occupied
the hilltops and an avalanche of shadows

fallen and engulfed the market place,
snuffing out the blue delphiniums. Yes,
things change. That they do so was something
you could always count on, and there was,
she supposed, comfort of a sort in that.

> The latter falls in love, and
> reads Spinoza . . .
>   *T. S. Eliot*

It was of course a joy for her to hear
the trumpets of the daffodils blare out
so brazenly around the house each spring.
It never had occurred to her to touch them though,
whereas, with tulips, their smooth round firmnesses
she couldn't help but stroke, softly and gently
with the backs of her fingers, from tip to stem,
the rich deep colours waxed so gorgeously.

Dull old Dr Johnson had said something,
hadn't he once, about not counting
the streaks inside a tulip? It wasn't
to be done, but she thought she would
to see if like the speckled patterns
in the gorge of foxgloves there were never
any two the same, like it was claimed
of snowflakes, which was a hard one to believe.

No, it wasn't getting any easier
these days, seeing things for what they were,
but then that Jew who fled from Portugal –
the one who polished lenses, wrote a treatise
on the rainbow and reasoned that *a free man thinks*
of nothing less than death, he never understood,
when he got to Amsterdam, why it was
the onions tasted so insipid there.

Now it may well be, in the long history
of our crowded universe, that her joy
or lack of joy, were two infinitesimally
small events, but this was her table in her
kitchen, and this was the chipped blue vase
her mother gave her; the tulips had all come
out of her own garden, and she did
so love the moist and silky feel to them.

Chapel Island is the first you come to
walking your way along the beach the full
length of the peninsular, a blessed relief
once for those who crossed these sands on foot,
boasting, so the story goes, its own
chantry for souls. Now even its folly's falling.

Next comes Foulney, then Piel, where poor little
Lambert Simnel landed, and at the very end
there's Walney, with its eider duck and terns;
sea-holly growing in the shingle, heart's ease
up in the dunes, and everywhere tight pink
dabs of the old threepenny-bit's thrift.

But it's not that. Something always draws me
to the tideline: that mess of stuff the waves
abandon – jettison – when they're forced
to admit defeat, to cower, crouch
and crawl back where they came from.
Mooching along, I could be taken

for some sort of beachcomber, but I'm not.
I don't have to do it. I'm not
looking for driftwood I can chop up
to keep me warm somewhere all winter,
nor do I expect or hope to find
a message in a bottle, or to chance

on something rich and rare, dropped
overboard one careless moonlit night
when her mind was elsewhere. This is
what the sea barfed, and I know
that among the twists and coils of blue
and orange nylon rope, the khaki

tentacles of weed clutching at condoms
and Pepsi bottles, the best I can hope
to find out here will be shells:
flanged cockles, blue–black mussels
and those pink half-moon shaped ones
that look like little fingernails.

Maybe a sea urchin if I'm lucky.
Always I know I'll pick up something
and take it home with me. I have to.
It's not that they're mementoes or even
talismans. I think it's that the sea
has always bothered me. It seems so

like the edge of the beyond, the chaos
our desire for order hurls itself against.
Coming and going, there's no coping with such
violent and controlled discord. I suppose I'm
always hoping one day it will have left behind
something to explain itself. It could be that.

IV

Ursa Major

Who, and why, that's what I'd
like to know, unable to sleep
one night, and lying back
under the stars, his hands cupped
behind his head, looked up
at six or seven of the brightest
and joining them together
in his mind the way a child might
in its dot-to-dot and colouring book,
instead of deciding, as would
have been only sensible
that it was shaped somewhat like
a watering-can or a soup ladle,
came up with the most improbable
of notions, viz that what he had
drawn was not simply *a*
but was *the* Great Bear?

Ridiculous.

But, bear, get your own back,
why don't you? Why not,
one morning, in those moments
before dawn, while Sirius and Leo
and all the others are fading
around you, re-assemble yourself
and step down awesomely among us,
setting one huge hind paw
on the top of Skiddaw,
the other, say, on Blencathra,
and raising your black
muzzle to the sky, give a
great shake to that sleek
brown rippling fur of yours?

Fill it with light. Roar
a little at us even
should you so wish to,
but be for us so much
more than bear, then, bear,
be thou Ursa Major.

THE BLESSED FOOL

Of the generation of the third son
he is – one of those whom we find it all too easy
to disparage, while we still
have the one with the brains,
and his brother with the muscles
to see us through when trouble comes.

But it isn't only in fables
that these two have unloosed
such a frenzy through their failures
that the heresy of the fool
was all we had to turn to: his modest
and yet inviolable quiet of the spirit.

It may then be only wise, with the old
ceremonies drifting into atrophy,
to reinvent the great Feast Day
of All Fools: to set it aside
as a time for the piling of irrational gifts
on the doorsteps of strangers;

as a day for the veneration of doodlers
and dreamers; and when evening comes,
one might perhaps invite the Fool himself
to dance for us, with steps
and gestures of an awkward
tenderness, his understanding of sorrow.

ICON

The welts and weals that puckered up his skin
showed where they'd laid the whip into him,
but the split lip, the bruises and the swellings
round his eyes told you this was a man
who'd been badly beaten up; 'scourged'
was hardly the word for what they'd done to him.

It was a picture, she said, she could not
take her eyes from: the inescapable
brutality of the incarnation;
godhead brought down by the darker
nature of man. And I knew what she meant.
Not that I knew her picture, but had

met up once perhaps with its perfect
opposite, when I bought an icon
that would not take its eyes off me.
Restrained, though brilliant in its browns
and gold, it portrayed so little
yet evoked so much; being not simply

an image, but a witness to the fact
of the image, there was no need
for any play of emotion, no light
or shadow. When I saw it first
its stillness was what moved, and still is
most strongly there for all its absences.

It's on the right, no more than a yard or so
before High Sunbrick Farm as you come up
over Birkrigg from Ulverston. In truth though,
when you get there, there isn't anything to see:
just another scrubby little paddock
behind a drystone wall; a bed of nettles,
a few thistles. But a plaque by the gate
says this was once a Quaker Burial Ground
and Margaret Fox (née Fell) was buried here.

But that's all. There never was a headstone
to show exactly where. For the Friends, the body
being at best but a dark lantern
to the inner light of the soul, to draw
attention to it would have seemed like vanity,
and that, they knew, was only one step short
of wantonness. And now I think of it,
I told a wanton lie myself when I said
there wasn't anything to see up here.

What's sure to stop you stone dead in your tracks
is the Parkers' whim of keeping peacocks
on their farm. Flaunting those plumed tiaras
on their heads, they must be the swaggering
antithesis of everything that Sunbrick
and the Man in Leather Breeches entertained
when they spread their tails, flutter
the lustrous iridescence of those eyes,
and dance their stately, slow pavan.

It's doubtful whether Margaret ever danced,
but it's to be hoped she saw the way the light
catches Bardsea steeplehouse as the dark
rain clouds come bruising their underbellies
over Ingleborough; and the changing
patterns of their shadows on the wet sands;
and those autumn evenings when the sunset
the far side of the bay looks like slices
of peaches. It is to be hoped she did.

THE FOUR HORSES

I

A white horse fidgets on a hill,
tilts one hind hoof forward,
then settles. The rider fusses gently
with its mane; shifts a little in his saddle.
Both are beginning to lose interest
in the fires and carnage in the valley.

II

If there was ever a time when the sun
was the flank of a blood-red horse
galloping down over the rim of the world,
it was seeing these men grinning and shoving in
to be photographed around the corpse
of a man they'd all but flayed.

III

'One measure of wheat for a penny!'
Hawkers and tinkers from way back
they'd been, the whole family, he said.
Times might, it's true, look bad, but thanks be
they still had Shadow – bonny nag – and the cart.
And it was a job needed doing: 'Bring out your dead!'

IV

Their fires spent, these sit on in darkness,
a defeated people. Obstinately alive,
they cough and shiver. Outside, drifts of snow
crouch, then scurry about their houses.
Soon the last of the riders will arrive,
reining in his pale horse at their door.

Though nothing but a shadow of itself,
there never was the shadow of a doubt
it was the fossil of a crocodile
they had unearthed in Kettleness. At first sight,
with its bones and scales perfectly intact,
it looked to her as if it had been stitched
inside the stone, an ancient petroglyph
somehow become embroidery.

Then Sunday came, and the truths of scripture
took a hammer to geology: *though they be hid*
in the bottom of the sea, thence will I command
my serpent and he will bite them; preached
with scarcely a thought for the women
whose menfolk might even then have been tumbling
through a tangled welter of rigging and spars,
past blunt, grey fish, to the sea's floor.

Sensing that she was beginning to skitter
and slide a little down Caedmon's Trod
in her hurry to get away from there,
she steadied herself and took a hold of the wall,
let herself gradually become aware
of the wind on her face, the clamour
and shriek of the gulls, and the little Whitby cobbles
going about their business in the harbour.

Twenty million years ago, they said, it lived here,
and she could picture them – a great plume of years
stretching out behind her like a comet's tail.
But with so few, she had begun to fear, still left
ahead of her, what use were they, any more
than these new continents that men had blundered on,
when day by day and year by year she'd sat,
sewing at this same window and in this same chair?

What Do We Have But Hope? was the motto,
set within a frieze of gaudy birds and flowers,
she'd worked at as a child. First one stitch
and then another she unpicked until
every one of them was gone. She did toy
with the notion of using her one last strand
of dark green silk to form, in tiny
running stitches, the knuckled outline

of the crocodile, but it was getting dark.
October had already come and gone,
tipping the black spot into the yellowing
outstretched palms of the sycamore that grew
behind the house. Rain rapped at the glass,
and there was a sigh from the wind as though
trying to tell her things which she was
by no means certain she had any wish to hear.

V

One

Almost the last, their Christmas card, all guilt
with angels, brought tidings of his coming death;
but eastwards towards Norwich I went, bearing gifts
of gloves and paperbacks and soap; wishing
I could share her confident: *all manner
of things shall be well.* Poor sparrow . . .

Edwin himself, that bitter Yule-tide in the mead-hall,
couldn't be sure whether it had been a thane's
gift with words, or if he'd really seen it
fluttering past him in the firelight.
Either way, the blizzard bared its teeth.
'No one gets out of life alive.'

Two

Just as there may be a river we've never reached
but know for sure to be there from the twists
and turns in a distant line of willows,
so the insinuations of a reality we cannot face
the mind explores and re-creates
in images: Acheron, Lethe, Styx.

And isn't it then through the lyricisms
of loss that we begin to sense
the tenderness of impermanence?
You remember how we saw the New Year in
at Baycliff, by the water's edge, while the slow
constellations wheeled on by overhead?

Three

What with the soil frozen so hard – stones
impacted like molars – you could hone
a scythe on my front garden this morning:
yet for all that, six or seven green
spathes of snowdrop have somehow slid themselves
through with not a mark on them.

Delicate deceivers. We look out for them
time after time, as though we were a part
of that world of renewal and return;
in hope whereof last year she interlaced
his winter-fingers with their pale heads
to carry with him through into the dark.

Four

In the brown depths – lustrous as seaweed –
of my daughter's eyes, I remember
my mother's; and in the opportunities
of the one: San Francisco, Istanbul,
realise now the frustrations – sheets to wash
and shopping to carry – of the other.

Midway between them, I would, as things go,
expect when I die to be fairly content
with the way things went; but conscious still
of the faint shadow of an only son –
so only as to have miscarried
before we had chance to set eyes on one another.

Five

There was this man coming home from work.
Simon his name was. Not looking for trouble.
If he'd thought on he'd have gone the other way
and not got mixed up in any of it,
but the centurion, he said, 'Hey, you, buggerlugs,
give him a hand with that; he can't cope with it.'

It was some terrorist too. Well, anyway,
that was why when he did get home his clothes
were all mussed up and there was this great bruise
on his shoulder. Said he didn't want to talk
about it; except he did say you never can tell
just when something's going to come and clobber you.

Six

The pollen checks looked hopeful: a type of
desert tamarix, native to Palestine;
the fear was carbon-14 tests
coming up with a date of fourteen hundred
and proving it fake. How then to believe
what our eyes had seen: the body of a man

scourged and crowned with thorns and crucified?
That such a death was not unique was not the point.
The miracle lay surely in what else we saw:
the folded hands, the dignity, the peace
and the awesome serenity of that face:
that this too was a man – *in imaginem dei.*

Seven

Not death, but the dying. It was raining
and the streets were thick with mud when they dragged
Campion on a hurdle from the Tower to Tyburn,
where they hanged him, cut him down alive, chopped off
his privy parts, disembowelled and beheaded him,
then hacked what was left into quarters.

For Margot, death came in the private ward
of a Barrow hospital. First one leg
then the other they amputated.
Mercifully unconsciousness had intervened.
She had no teeth in and was incontinent.
If only I had made it to her funeral.

Eight

A child's face lies among the shoes
and second-hand dresses on a stall.
This was Sarajevo's 'Massacre
of the Market Place' – alliteration
soothing it towards fiction and oblivion.
But the past persists. It is where

precedents take place; though God alone
knows what new hell this could presage?
'Weep for your children,' he told the daughters
of Jerusalem, 'for if they do these things
in a green tree, what shall be done in the dry?'
His assumption being there would still be trees.

Nine

Eager for coherence, I am always
gladdened by the mind's ability
to make beauty – if not sense –
out of the teeming particularities
that strafe us like meteorites;
but events of late have proved a problem:

it's not just recession, terrorist attacks
and toxic spillage; there were those mudslides
after the earthquake; fraud, scandal and theft;
bushfires, shipwrecks; and deaths of course
by various and gruesome kinds of violence.
What Lent can follow such a Mardi Gras?

Ten

Memory teaches us to remember
(There was snow on the beach, and ice. The sea
had gone, leaving this token of itself behind)
but no one as yet has found the way to forget.
The future you might expect to arrive
like an incoming tide; but this tide's been here before.

This is no sacrament to wash us clean.
The old rope and guilt, the humiliation
and plastic we flung into it yesterday
comes back again. This is our inheritance.
The past will drench us in our own detritus.
Waves strip the bone white and leave it on the shore.

Eleven

If I'd dared to prise open his hands
I'd have seen the pale half-moons his fingernails
had made where he'd been clenching them so hard.
That would have told me something. I could have gone
with him to the water's edge and walked
by his side (these fourteen steps at least)

watching the smoke-grey ripples of sea-snipe
turning to silver; hearing the curlews cry
among the dunes and in the shallows; and this
before he left for where the white gannets wheel
and soar, stretching their slim wings out wide
against the sky as they turn and dive   dive   dive

Twelve

When the bleep stops and the green line lies down flat
on the electroencephalograph –
that's death. It used to be held to be breath:
breathing out the air we'd breathed in at our birth.
'This feather stirs; she lives!' but Lear was wrong,
Cordelia's breath would mist no stone again.

Heart-breaking? And a heart-break that must feel
as physical as the fingers on the wrist
where no pulse beats. But it's the head
against the heart that tells us – the phenomena
of the mind – and ultimately in the mind
of whichever of us is left behind to grieve.

Thirteen

Yes. Yes, you can. You can imagine it.
It's like when you take an uncooked chicken
out of the fridge – well perhaps not quite so cold –
that's the way a corpse feels – and it's not nice.
You know straight away something's missing,
something we conspire to call: life.

And yet – as with the pietà – that kiss,
sweet to the lips if bitter to the taste,
love has never flinched from. Our feelings
for the dead don't fade because they're dead:
they fade because we ourselves are losing
in the struggle against impermanence.

Fourteen

Mindful of the ships in bottles he had made –
cold rain splattering into the grave –
I smashed one to pieces on a tombstone,
set fire to the bowsprit and the rigging,
and with himself lying in state on the quarterdeck
sent it sailing proudly away down the runnels . . .

Just once to have countered dust and ashes
with: And thus they buried Hector, tamer of horses;
or: Winter has passed, *et flores*
apparuerunt in terra nostra – by some such
attestation of worth at least
to make peace with the certitude of loss.